WORKBOOK

For

The Christ Cure

10 Biblical Ways to Heal from Trauma, Tragedy, and PTSD

[A Guide to Implementing Tim Murphy's Book]

Kelly Press

Table of Content

How To Use This Workbook

This workbook provides you with the chance to investigate a variety of aspects of your life, identify areas in need of improvement, and observe your advancement. It has a compilation of essential topics, questions to stimulate contemplation, and learning review questions to gauge your progression.

To ensure you stay on track and make progress, it's advised that you establish a timeline for completing the workbook. Set aside specific periods to work through the prompts and learning review questions. This will help you maintain your momentum and ensure you make steady progress.

The workbook commences with a short recap of the main book, acquainting you with the topic discussed in the title. This approach is highly beneficial for obtaining a deeper understanding of the content covered in the workbook, as well as identifying the areas that require the most attention.

The key lessons and the action prompts provided in this workbook aim to inspire contemplation on various facets of your life. You need not respond to all of them simultaneously and may revisit them later. They serve as a base for your self-reflection and personal exploration.

Once you complete the activities in this workbook, you can assess your progress by answering self-assessment questions. The purpose of these questions is to prompt you to reflect on your learning and identify which areas you need to focus on more. Armed with this knowledge, you can devise effective strategies to enhance your comprehension of the material.

Feel free to spend enough time on the prompts and self-assessment questions. You do not need to finish them in one go. You can take a pause and come back to them later. The most significant thing is to be truthful to yourself and to give careful thought to your responses.

Good luck!

Kelly Press

Overview

Tim Murphy's book, The Christ Cure, discusses the confluence of Christianity and trauma rehabilitation. The author draws on his expertise as a former military chaplain and therapist to present a thorough approach to trauma treatment based on biblical principles.

The book is organized into ten chapters, each of which focuses on a distinct component of trauma rehabilitation. The first chapter establishes the context by analyzing the prevalence of trauma and PTSD in modern culture, as well as the significance of approaching these challenges via a biblical lens. Murphy contends that Christians are especially suited to deal with trauma because they believe in a compassionate, merciful, and powerful God.

In the following chapters, the author digs into specific biblical themes and practices that can aid in trauma healing. Prayer, forgiveness, fellowship, appreciation, hope, and worship are examples of these. Murphy uses personal experiences as well as scriptural examples to demonstrate how these principles might be implemented in real-world situations.

The book's emphasis on the significance of community in trauma rehabilitation is one of its distinguishing features. Murphy contends that recovery cannot occur in isolation and that trauma sufferers must seek support and encouragement from those who share their religion. He also offers tips on how to build a supportive community, including ideas for small group activities and strategies to promote deeper relationships.

Murphy highlights the significance of receiving professional support for trauma recovery throughout the book. He admits that, while biblical ideas can be beneficial, they are not a replacement for therapy or medical care. He also provides information on how to identify qualified therapists and support groups.

The Christ Cure is a thorough trauma rehabilitation guide that blends biblical ideas with practical counsel. It will be especially beneficial for Christians dealing with trauma and PTSD, but it is also a useful resource for anybody interested in learning more about the connection between faith and mental health.

Part One: Trauma Is Everywhere

You Are Not Owned by Trauma

Key Lessons

1. Trauma does not define you. It is a part of your story, but it does not have to be the defining part.

2. It is possible to move beyond the pain and find healing from trauma. This process requires patience, perseverance, and a willingness to seek help.

3. Finding meaning and purpose in your trauma can help you transcend it. This may involve using your experience to help others or finding a way to turn your pain into something positive.

4. Forgiveness is a powerful tool for healing from trauma. By letting go of anger and bitterness, you can free yourself from the hold that trauma has on your life.

5. Ultimately, healing from trauma requires a shift in mindset. Instead of being a victim, you can choose to be a survivor and use your experience to grow stronger and more resilient.

Action Prompts

How do you currently define yourself in relation to your trauma? Is it possible to shift this definition?

_____

_____

_____

_____

_____

_____

_____

_____

_____

_____

_____

_____

_____

_____

What are some steps you can take to move beyond the pain of your trauma and find healing?

_____

_____

_____

_____

_____

_____

_____

_____

_____

_____

_____

_____

_____

_____

How can you find meaning or purpose in your trauma? Are there any ways you can use your experience to help others?

_____

_____

_____

_____

_____

_____

_____

_____

_____

_____

_____

_____

_____

_____

Is there someone you need to forgive in order to move forward from your trauma? How can you work on letting go of anger and bitterness?

_____

_____

_____

_____

_____

_____

_____

_____

_____

_____

_____

_____

_____

What mindset shifts can you make to move from being a victim of trauma to a survivor? What are some ways you can grow stronger and more resilient?

_____

_____

_____

_____

_____

_____

_____

_____

_____

_____

_____

_____

_____

_____

What role does faith play in your healing journey? How can you use your faith to find strength and hope in the midst of trauma?

_____

_____

_____

_____

_____

_____

_____

_____

_____

_____

_____

_____

_____

_____

How can you create a support system of friends, family, or professionals to help you on your healing journey? What steps can you take to build this community around you?

_____

_____

_____

_____

_____

_____

_____

_____

_____

_____

Trauma Does Leave a Mark

Key Lessons

1. Trauma changes the brain and affects the way we process information, which can result in symptoms such as anxiety, depression, and hypervigilance.

2. Trauma can also affect our physical health, leading to issues such as chronic pain, cardiovascular disease, and autoimmune disorders.

3. Trauma can affect our relationships by causing us to isolate ourselves or become overly dependent on others.

4. Trauma can be passed down through generations, leading to intergenerational trauma that can affect entire families or communities.

5. It is possible to recover from trauma and heal from its effects, but it requires intentional effort and a willingness to seek help and support from others.

Action Prompts

How has trauma affected your mental and physical health?

_____

_____

_____

_____

_____

_____

_____

_____

_____

_____

_____

_____

_____

In what ways has trauma affected your relationships with others?

_____

_____

_____

_____

_____

_____

_____

_____

_____

_____

_____

_____

_____

_____

Have you noticed any patterns of trauma or adversity in your family history?

_____

_____

_____

_____

_____

_____

_____

_____

_____

_____

_____

_____

_____

What steps are you currently taking to heal from trauma, and what additional support might you need?

_____

_____

_____

_____

_____

_____

_____

_____

_____

_____

_____

_____

How has your faith or spirituality helped you cope with trauma?

_____

_____

_____

_____

_____

_____

_____

_____

_____

_____

_____

_____

_____

_____

_____

What strategies have you found helpful for managing symptoms of trauma, such as anxiety or hypervigilance?

_____

_____

_____

_____

_____

_____

_____

_____

_____

_____

_____

_____

_____

_____

_____

In what ways can you use your own experiences of trauma to help others who may be going through similar experiences?

_____

_____

_____

_____

_____

_____

_____

_____

_____

_____

_____

_____

How Trauma Affects You

Key Lessons

1. Trauma can have long-lasting effects on your physical, emotional, and spiritual health. Trauma can manifest itself in a variety of ways, including physical symptoms like headaches or stomach problems, emotional symptoms like anxiety or depression, and spiritual symptoms like a sense of disconnection from God.

2. Trauma can impact your relationships with others. Trauma survivors may struggle with trust, intimacy, and communication, which can strain their relationships with friends and family members. It's important to be patient and understanding with yourself and others as you navigate these challenges.

3. Trauma can affect your worldview and sense of self. Trauma can lead to feelings of shame, guilt, and worthlessness, which can impact how you see yourself and the world around you. It's important to recognize these feelings and work to replace them with more positive, accurate beliefs.

4. Trauma can impact your ability to regulate your emotions. Trauma survivors may struggle with emotional regulation, experiencing intense emotions like anger or fear in response to seemingly minor triggers. It's important to learn healthy coping mechanisms for managing your emotions.

5. Trauma can be healed with time, support, and effective treatment. While trauma can have long-lasting effects, it is possible to find healing and recovery with the right tools and support.

Action Prompts

In what ways has trauma impacted your physical, emotional, or spiritual health? How can you work to address these impacts?

_____

_____

_____

_____

_____

_____

_____

_____

_____

_____

_____

_____

_____

How has trauma affected your relationships with others? What steps can you take to rebuild trust and connection with loved ones?

_____

_____

_____

_____

_____

_____

_____

_____

_____

_____

_____

_____

_____

_____

_____

How has trauma impacted your sense of self and worldview? What beliefs do you need to let go of, and what new beliefs can you adopt to promote healing and growth?

_____

_____

_____

_____

_____

_____

_____

_____

_____

_____

_____

_____

_____

_____

_____

How do you currently cope with intense emotions? Are there healthier coping mechanisms you can adopt?

_____

_____

_____

_____

_____

_____

_____

_____

_____

_____

_____

_____

_____

_____

What support systems do you currently have in place for healing from trauma? Are there additional resources or forms of support you can seek out?

_____

_____

_____

_____

_____

_____

_____

_____

_____

_____

_____

_____

_____

How can you practice patience and understanding with yourself as you navigate the challenges of trauma recovery?

_____

_____

_____

_____

_____

_____

_____

_____

_____

_____

_____

_____

_____

_____

_____

What steps can you take to prioritize your physical, emotional, and spiritual health as you work towards healing from trauma?

_____

_____

_____

_____

_____

_____

_____

_____

_____

_____

Part Two: Steps to Healing

Step 1 - Build Your Own Resilience

Key Lessons

1. Resilience is the ability to bounce back from adversity and trauma, and it can be strengthened through intentional effort and practice.

2. Developing resilience requires cultivating a positive outlook, learning from mistakes, and building a support network of friends and family.

3. It is important to set realistic goals and prioritize self-care activities like exercise, healthy eating, and rest in order to maintain physical and emotional health.

4. Nurturing spiritual practices such as prayer, worship, and reading the Bible can provide a sense of meaning and purpose that helps build resilience.

5. Resilience is not a fixed trait, but rather a dynamic process that can be improved over time with consistent effort and intentional focus.

Action Prompts

In what ways have you demonstrated resilience in the past, and how can you build on these experiences to strengthen your ability to cope with future challenges?

_____

_____

_____

_____

_____

_____

_____

_____

_____

_____

_____

_____

_____

What are some realistic goals you can set for yourself to promote physical and emotional well-being, and how can you ensure that you prioritize self-care activities in your daily routine?

_____

_____

_____

_____

_____

_____

_____

_____

_____

_____

_____

_____

_____

How can you cultivate a more positive outlook on life, even in the midst of adversity and trauma?

_____

_____

_____

_____

_____

_____

_____

_____

_____

_____

_____

_____

_____

_____

_____

What spiritual practices have you found helpful in the past, and how can you incorporate them into your daily routine to cultivate a sense of purpose and meaning?

_____

_____

_____

_____

_____

_____

_____

_____

_____

_____

_____

_____

_____

_____

_____

What mistakes have you made in the past, and how can you learn from them in order to become more resilient?

_____

_____

_____

_____

_____

_____

_____

_____

_____

_____

_____

_____

How can you build a stronger support network of friends and family who can provide encouragement and support during difficult times?

_____

_____

_____

_____

_____

_____

_____

_____

_____

_____

_____

_____

_____

_____

What steps can you take to cultivate a growth mindset and view challenges as opportunities for learning and personal growth rather than as insurmountable obstacles?

_____

_____

_____

_____

_____

_____

_____

_____

_____

_____

Step 2 - Arm Yourself with Resilience

Key Lessons

1. Resilience is a skill that can be developed and strengthened through intentional practice and a willingness to persevere through challenges.

2. One important aspect of resilience is the ability to reframe negative experiences and find meaning and purpose in adversity.

3. Practicing gratitude and focusing on blessings can help build resilience by fostering a positive outlook and reducing stress.

4. Developing a sense of purpose and mission can provide motivation and direction during difficult times.

5. Engaging in regular self-care practices, such as exercise and meditation, can help build physical and emotional resilience.

Action Prompts

How do you typically respond to adversity? Do you tend to give up easily or persevere through challenges?

_____

_____

_____

_____

_____

_____

_____

_____

_____

_____

_____

_____

_____

How can you reframe a negative experience in your life to find meaning and purpose in it?

_____

_____

_____

_____

_____

_____

_____

_____

_____

_____

_____

_____

_____

_____

_____

What are some blessings in your life that you can focus
on to help build resilience and reduce stress?

_____

_____

_____

_____

_____

_____

_____

_____

_____

_____

_____

_____

_____

_____

_____

What is your sense of purpose or mission in life, and how can you use this to motivate you during difficult times?

_____

_____

_____

_____

_____

_____

_____

_____

_____

_____

_____

_____

_____

_____

What self-care practices do you currently engage in, and how can you prioritize them to build physical and emotional resilience?

_____

_____

_____

_____

_____

_____

_____

_____

_____

_____

_____

_____

_____

_____

_____

What are some examples of people you know who
exhibit strong resilience, and what can you learn from
them?

_____

_____

_____

_____

_____

_____

_____

_____

_____

_____

_____

_____

_____

_____

How can you intentionally practice building resilience in your everyday life? What steps can you take to develop this skill?

_____

_____

_____

_____

_____

_____

_____

_____

_____

_____

_____

_____

_____

Step 3 - Embrace Your Recovery

Key Lessons

1. Healing is a process, and it's important to acknowledge that it takes time and effort. You can't rush your recovery, but you can make the choice to actively participate in it.

2. Recovery requires a willingness to face your pain and to confront the emotions and memories that come with it. It may be uncomfortable or even painful, but it's a necessary part of the healing process.

3. One important aspect of recovery is learning to let go of control and trusting in God's plan for your life. This may involve surrendering your expectations and accepting that your recovery journey may look different from what you imagined.

4. It's essential to have a support system in place as you work towards recovery. This may include family, friends, a therapist, or a support group. Building a community of people who understand and care about your struggles can be a powerful tool for healing.

5. Recovery is not a linear process, and setbacks are to be expected. It's important to be gentle with yourself and to not give up hope. With persistence and perseverance, healing is possible.

Action Prompts

How have you been approaching your recovery process?
Are you willing to put in the time and effort necessary to
heal?

_____

_____

_____

_____

_____

_____

_____

_____

_____

_____

_____

_____

What emotions or memories are you avoiding that may
be preventing you from fully embracing your recovery?

_____

_____

_____

_____

_____

_____

_____

_____

_____

_____

_____

_____

_____

_____

In what ways do you struggle with letting go of control and trusting in God's plan? How can you work on surrendering your expectations?

_____

_____

_____

_____

_____

_____

_____

_____

_____

_____

_____

_____

_____

_____

Who is in your support system, and how have they been
helping you in your recovery journey? Are there
additional resources or people you could seek out for
support?

_____

_____

_____

_____

_____

_____

_____

_____

_____

_____

_____

_____

_____

How do you typically respond to setbacks or difficulties in your recovery? What steps can you take to be more resilient and persistent?

_____

_____

_____

_____

_____

_____

_____

_____

_____

_____

_____

_____

Are there any patterns or habits in your life that may be hindering your recovery? How can you make changes to support your healing?

_____

_____

_____

_____

_____

_____

_____

_____

_____

_____

_____

_____

_____

What small steps can you take today to actively participate in your recovery process and move closer to healing?

_____

_____

_____

_____

_____

_____

_____

_____

_____

_____

Step 4 - Accept Your Renewal

Key Lessons

1. Renewal is an ongoing process: Renewal is not a one-time event but a continuous process of growth and change. It is essential to accept that healing from trauma takes time and that there will be setbacks along the way.

2. Renewal requires vulnerability: Healing from trauma involves acknowledging and processing painful emotions. It is essential to be vulnerable and honest with yourself and others about your experiences to move forward.

3. Renewal involves surrendering control: Trauma can lead to a sense of loss of control, and the process of renewal requires surrendering that sense of control and trusting in God's plan for your life.

4. Renewal requires an open mind: Be open to learning new things and challenging old beliefs about yourself and your trauma. Embrace the opportunity for growth and change.

5. Renewal is grounded in faith: Trusting in God and turning to Him for guidance is essential in the process of renewal. Faith provides a foundation of

hope and a source of strength during difficult times.

Action Prompts

In what ways have you resisted the process of renewal and healing from trauma?

_____

_____

_____

_____

_____

_____

_____

_____

_____

_____

_____

_____

_____

How has vulnerability played a role in your healing process? What areas do you still struggle to be vulnerable in?

_____

_____

_____

_____

_____

_____

_____

_____

_____

_____

_____

_____

_____

_____

What areas of your life do you struggle to surrender control over? How can you begin to trust God's plan for your life?

_____

_____

_____

_____

_____

_____

_____

_____

_____

_____

_____

_____

_____

_____

Are you open to learning new things and challenging old beliefs about yourself and your trauma? How can you embrace the opportunity for growth and change?

_____

_____

_____

_____

_____

_____

_____

_____

_____

_____

_____

_____

_____

How has your faith helped you in the process of renewal and healing from trauma? In what ways can you deepen your trust in God?

_____

_____

_____

_____

_____

_____

_____

_____

_____

_____

_____

_____

What steps can you take to create a supportive community that will encourage and support your renewal process?

_____

_____

_____

_____

_____

_____

_____

_____

_____

_____

_____

_____

_____

_____

What can you do to remind yourself that renewal is an ongoing process and that setbacks are a normal part of the healing journey?

_____

_____

_____

_____

_____

_____

_____

_____

_____

_____

_____

Part Three: Six Steps to STAY Healthy

Step 5 - Get Fit

Key Lessons

1. Exercise is a powerful tool for healing trauma, as it releases endorphins and helps regulate mood and sleep patterns.

2. Consistency is key when it comes to exercise, and it's important to find activities that you enjoy and that fit into your schedule.

3. Physical health and spiritual health are interconnected, and taking care of your body is a form of worship.

4. Exercise can help build resilience and increase self-esteem, both of which are important for healing from trauma.

5. It's important to approach exercise with a positive mindset, focusing on what your body can do rather than what it can't, and avoiding negative self-talk.

Action Prompts

How often do you exercise, and what are some ways you could incorporate more movement into your daily routine?

_____

_____

_____

_____

_____

_____

_____

_____

_____

_____

_____

_____

_____

What physical activities do you enjoy, and how could you make time for them in your schedule?

_____

_____

_____

_____

_____

_____

_____

_____

_____

_____

_____

_____

_____

_____

How do you view the connection between your physical and spiritual health, and what role does exercise play in that connection?

_____

_____

_____

_____

_____

_____

_____

_____

_____

_____

_____

_____

_____

_____

In what ways has exercise helped you build resilience or increase your self-esteem?

_____

_____

_____

_____

_____

_____

_____

_____

_____

_____

_____

_____

Do you ever struggle with negative self-talk when it comes to your body or your ability to exercise? If so, how could you reframe those thoughts in a more positive way?

_____

_____

_____

_____

_____

_____

_____

_____

_____

_____

_____

_____

_____

What are some potential barriers to starting or maintaining an exercise routine, and how could you overcome those barriers?

_____

_____

_____

_____

_____

_____

_____

_____

_____

_____

_____

_____

_____

How could you involve others in your exercise routine,
whether by joining a group fitness class or working out
with a friend or family member, and how might this
benefit your overall health and well-being?

_____

_____

_____

_____

_____

_____

_____

_____

_____

_____

_____

_____

_____

_____

Step 6 - Strengthen Your Attitudes

Key Lessons

1. Positive attitudes can be developed through intentional effort, and they are essential for maintaining mental and emotional health.

2. Cultivating an attitude of gratitude can help shift focus from negative experiences to positive ones, and increase resilience in the face of adversity.

3. Forgiveness is an important attitude to cultivate, as holding onto bitterness and anger can lead to negative physical and emotional consequences.

4. Humility and a willingness to learn from others can help individuals maintain a growth mindset and continue to develop their attitudes over time.

5. Attitudes can be strengthened through regular prayer and reflection on biblical principles.

Action Prompts

How can you intentionally cultivate a positive attitude in your daily life?

_____

_____

_____

_____

_____

_____

_____

_____

_____

_____

_____

_____

In what ways have you seen gratitude impact your mental and emotional health?

_____

_____

_____

_____

_____

_____

_____

_____

_____

_____

_____

_____

_____

_____

Are there areas in your life where you struggle with forgiveness? How can you work towards cultivating a more forgiving attitude?

_____

_____

_____

_____

_____

_____

_____

_____

_____

_____

_____

_____

_____

_____

How can you remain humble and open to learning from others, even in situations where you may feel confident in your own knowledge or experience?

_____

_____

_____

_____

_____

_____

_____

_____

_____

_____

_____

_____

How does regular prayer and reflection on biblical principles impact your attitudes towards yourself and others?

_____

_____

_____

_____

_____

_____

_____

_____

_____

_____

_____

_____

_____

What attitudes do you currently hold that may be hindering your mental and emotional health? How can you work towards shifting these attitudes?

_____

_____

_____

_____

_____

_____

_____

_____

_____

_____

_____

_____

_____

_____

How can you incorporate intentional attitude strengthening practices into your daily routine?

_____

_____

_____

_____

_____

_____

_____

_____

_____

_____

_____

_____

Step 7 - Get Enough Sleep

Key Lessons

1. Sleep is essential for physical and emotional health. Lack of sleep can cause irritability, decreased concentration, and even depression.

2. Establishing a consistent sleep routine is crucial for getting enough sleep. Going to bed and waking up at the same time every day can help regulate your body's sleep-wake cycle.

3. Avoiding caffeine, nicotine, and alcohol before bedtime can help improve the quality of your sleep.

4. Creating a comfortable sleep environment, such as using comfortable bedding and keeping the bedroom quiet and dark, can promote better sleep.

5. Praying before bed and cultivating a peaceful and grateful mindset can also help improve sleep quality.

Action Prompts

How consistent is your sleep routine, and what changes can you make to improve it?

_____

_____

_____

_____

_____

_____

_____

_____

_____

_____

_____

_____

_____

Do you avoid caffeine, nicotine, and alcohol before bedtime? If not, what changes can you make to improve your sleep quality?

_____

_____

_____

_____

_____

_____

_____

_____

_____

_____

_____

_____

_____

_____

What changes can you make to create a more comfortable sleep environment in your bedroom?

_____

_____

_____

_____

_____

_____

_____

_____

_____

_____

_____

_____

_____

_____

How often do you pray or cultivate a peaceful mindset
before bed, and how can you incorporate these practices
into your nightly routine?

_____

_____

_____

_____

_____

_____

_____

_____

_____

_____

_____

_____

_____

How has lack of sleep affected your physical and
emotional health in the past?

_____

_____

_____

_____

_____

_____

_____

_____

_____

_____

_____

_____

_____

_____

How do you prioritize sleep in your daily routine, and what adjustments can you make to ensure that you are getting enough sleep?

_____

_____

_____

_____

_____

_____

_____

_____

_____

_____

_____

_____

_____

_____

Are there any underlying mental health issues that may
be impacting your sleep, and what steps can you take to
address them?

_____

_____

_____

_____

_____

_____

_____

_____

_____

_____

_____

_____

_____

Step 8 - Train Your Mind

Key Lessons

1. Our thoughts have a significant impact on our emotions and behavior, and it's essential to train our minds to think positively and healthily.

2. We can train our minds by practicing gratitude, meditation, and focusing on positive affirmations from scripture.

3. Regular exercise and physical activity can also contribute to mental wellness and resilience.

4. It's crucial to identify and challenge negative self-talk and replace it with positive self-talk.

5. Consistency and perseverance are key to training our minds and developing healthy thought patterns.

Action Prompts

What negative thought patterns have you noticed in yourself, and how have they affected your emotions and behavior?

_____

_____

_____

_____

_____

_____

_____

_____

_____

_____

_____

_____

_____

What are some positive affirmations or Bible verses that resonate with you, and how can you incorporate them into your daily routine?

_____

_____

_____

_____

_____

_____

_____

_____

_____

_____

_____

_____

_____

How does physical activity contribute to your mental health and well-being, and what are some ways you can make it a regular part of your life?

_____

_____

_____

_____

_____

_____

_____

_____

_____

_____

_____

_____

_____

_____

What are some common negative self-talk phrases you use, and how can you challenge and replace them with positive self-talk?

_____

_____

_____

_____

_____

_____

_____

_____

_____

_____

_____

_____

_____

How consistent have you been in training your mind and developing healthy thought patterns, and what strategies can you use to stay motivated and committed?

_____

_____

_____

_____

_____

_____

_____

_____

_____

_____

_____

_____

_____

How have your past experiences and trauma shaped your current thought patterns, and what steps can you take to move towards healing and growth?

_____

_____

_____

_____

_____

_____

_____

_____

_____

_____

_____

_____

_____

_____

_____

How can you cultivate an attitude of gratitude in your
life, and what benefits do you think it would have on
your mental health and overall well-being?

_____

_____

_____

_____

_____

_____

_____

_____

_____

_____

_____

Step 9 - Eat Healthy

Key Lessons

1. The importance of eating whole, nutrient-dense foods to support physical and mental health.

2. The benefits of avoiding processed and sugary foods, which can contribute to inflammation and other health issues.

3. The role of hydration in maintaining physical and mental wellness.

4. The significance of mindful eating, which involves paying attention to hunger cues and savoring food.

5. The value of seeking support from a nutritionist or registered dietitian to create a personalized healthy eating plan.

Action Prompts

How often do you consume whole, nutrient-dense foods?
How can you incorporate more of these foods into your
diet?

_____

_____

_____

_____

_____

_____

_____

_____

_____

_____

_____

_____

What are some of your favorite processed or sugary
foods? How can you reduce your consumption of these
items?

_____

_____

_____

_____

_____

_____

_____

_____

_____

_____

_____

_____

_____

_____

Do you prioritize staying hydrated throughout the day? If not, what are some strategies you can use to increase your water intake?

_____

_____

_____

_____

_____

_____

_____

_____

_____

_____

_____

_____

_____

_____

How often do you eat mindfully, paying attention to
hunger cues and savoring your food? What are some
barriers to practicing mindful eating, and how can you
overcome them?

_____

_____

_____

_____

_____

_____

_____

_____

_____

_____

_____

_____

_____

Have you ever sought support from a nutritionist or registered dietitian? If not, what are some reasons you may consider doing so?

_____

_____

_____

_____

_____

_____

_____

_____

_____

_____

_____

_____

_____

How does your diet affect your mental health and well-being? Are there any changes you can make to support your mental health through your diet?

_____

_____

_____

_____

_____

_____

_____

_____

_____

_____

_____

_____

_____

_____

What are some practical steps you can take to maintain
healthy eating habits, even during times of stress or
trauma?

_____

_____

_____

_____

_____

_____

_____

_____

_____

_____

Step 10 - Learn to Relax

Key Lessons

1. Relaxation is essential for physical, mental, and emotional health, and it can be learned and practiced intentionally through techniques such as deep breathing, visualization, and muscle relaxation.

2. Relaxation can help manage symptoms of trauma and PTSD, such as anxiety, hypervigilance, and sleep disturbances, by calming the nervous system and promoting a sense of safety and well-being.

3. Regular relaxation practice can help reduce the risk of chronic stress-related illnesses, such as cardiovascular disease, diabetes, and autoimmune disorders, by lowering cortisol levels and boosting immune function.

4. Engaging in enjoyable, low-stress activities such as hobbies, sports, or socializing can also promote relaxation and well-being, as long as they are not used as a form of avoidance or distraction from unresolved trauma.

5. Cultivating a daily practice of relaxation and self-care is essential for maintaining long-term healing

and preventing relapse, and it requires patience, commitment, and self-compassion.

Action Prompts

What are some relaxation techniques that work best for you, and how often do you practice them?

_____

_____

_____

_____

_____

_____

_____

_____

_____

_____

_____

_____

_____

How do you know when you are feeling stressed or anxious, and what are some early warning signs that you need to take a break?

_____

_____

_____

_____

_____

_____

_____

_____

_____

_____

_____

_____

_____

_____

_____

_____

What are some enjoyable, low-stress activities that you would like to incorporate into your daily or weekly routine, and how can you make time for them?

_____

_____

_____

_____

_____

_____

_____

_____

_____

_____

_____

_____

_____

_____

_____

What are some common triggers or situations that make
it difficult for you to relax, and how can you prepare for
or cope with them more effectively?

_____

_____

_____

_____

_____

_____

_____

_____

_____

_____

_____

_____

_____

_____

How do you balance the need for relaxation and self-care with other responsibilities and obligations, such as work, family, or caregiving?

_____

_____

_____

_____

_____

_____

_____

_____

_____

_____

_____

_____

_____

What are some self-compassionate statements or affirmations that you can use to encourage yourself when you are feeling overwhelmed or discouraged in your healing journey?

_____

_____

_____

_____

_____

_____

_____

_____

_____

_____

_____

_____

_____

_____

How can you cultivate a sense of gratitude and appreciation for the progress you have made so far in your healing, while also acknowledging the challenges and setbacks that are a natural part of the process?

_____

_____

_____

_____

_____

_____

_____

_____

_____

Learning Review Questions

What made you purchase this workbook?

_____

_____

_____

_____

_____

_____

How have you been using the workbook so far?

_____

_____

_____

_____

_____

_____

What do you feel you have gained from using the workbook?

_____

_____

_____

_____

_____

_____

How has the workbook helped you to achieve your goals?

_____

_____

_____

_____

_____

_____

Are there any parts of the workbook that were particularly helpful or challenging for you?

_____

_____

_____

_____

_____

_____

How has your understanding or knowledge of the topic changed since working through the workbook?

_____

_____

_____

_____

_____

_____

_____

How do you plan to continue using the workbook or incorporating the information in your life?

_____

_____

_____

_____

_____

_____

_____

Made in the USA
Las Vegas, NV
02 December 2024

13155315R00059